For Nadine

In memory of Justin

HEALING THE ADULT
SIBLING'S GRIEVING HEART

I know your heart will
never be "Healed" but may
it get strong enough to
bear life as it now is.
May the memories be
happy ones that give
more comfort than
grief.
Love mum
XOXO

Companion Press is dedicated to the education and support of both the bereaved and bereavement caregivers.

We believe that those who companion the bereaved by walking with them as they journey in grief have a wondrous opportunity: to help others embrace and grow through grief—and to lead fuller, more deeply-lived lives themselves because of this important ministry.

For a complete catalog and ordering information, write or call:

Companion Press
The Center for Loss and Life Transition
3735 Broken Bow Road
Fort Collins, CO 80526
(970) 226-6050
www.centerforloss.com

HEALING THE ADULT SIBLING'S GRIEVING HEART

•

100 PRACTICAL IDEAS AFTER YOUR BROTHER OR SISTER DIES

•

ALAN D. WOLFELT, PH.D.

Fort Collins, Colorado
An imprint of the Center for Loss and Life Transition

Companion Press is an imprint of the
Center for Loss and Life Transition,
3735 Broken Bow Road, Fort Collins, Colorado 80526
970-226-6050
www.centerforloss.com

Companion Press books may be purchased in bulk for sales promotions, premiums or fundraisers. Please contact the publisher at the above address for more information.

Printed in the United States of America

11 10 09 08   5 4 3 2 1

ISBN: 978-1-879651-29-6

This book is lovingly dedicated in memory of Mitch Anderson.

Mitch Anderson and his sister, Amy

FOREWORD

Seven years ago, my life changed forever.

It started with the fateful phone call from my panic-stricken mother. I will never forget that conversation. The moment in time is as real now as it was that day. Her piercing words are still ringing in my ears. The scream that erupted from my own lungs is still vivid and painful. My exact location, my clothing, the weather and even the short drive I had in front of me is so real, as if it just happened.

Her words were, "Amy, your brother is dead."

And everything changed.

My future changed.

My past changed.

My life changed.

Forever.

My strong, intelligent, "on-top-of-the-world," entrepreneurial, well-liked, supportive, understanding, funny, charming, loving adult brother was gone. My best friend and confidant was gone. Forever. And my life would never be the same.

My dreams for him, for our future together, were gone. I would never have a sister-in-law, a niece or nephew, a large Christmas gathering full of family…my family. The reality that I was "it"— alone, the only child, the only person left to take care of our parents in the future—hit so hard. Not Mitch and I, as we had joked and teased about for years. Just me.

People often ask me how my parents are doing since Mitch's death. How my grandparents are doing. How my children are doing. And even how my brother's dog is doing. What they don't ask is how I'm doing. It's just understood that because I'm an adult, I'm dealing with this loss differently or more valiantly than others. Or perhaps it's that the relationship I had with Mitch was different than the relationships they share with their siblings. I'm not sure.

I do know this: I lost my "partner in crime," a person I don't remember life without, my best friend. I am blown away with emotion. I have a deep sadness for the things that will never be the same and for the thing I will never have with my brother. I miss the childhood validation I got from him and our long talks about what we looked forward to in the future.

It has been eight years since Mitch died, and I can say that my grief has softened. In the beginning, I couldn't talk about his life or death without crying and feeling gut-wrenchingly devastated. Now I'm more able to remember his life, not just his death.

What has helped me with my grief? Talking about him has been the biggest help. Every time I tell the stories of his life and death, my emotions get a little less raw and I feel a little stronger. In this book you'll see that Dr. Wolfelt advocates actively remembering your brother or sister who died. It's true. The more you remember, and the more you share those memories—good and bad—aloud with others, the more you will begin to heal.

My family also makes a point of remembering Mitch on special days. We tell stories about him on holidays and we honor him in other ways. For us, it helps to acknowledge Mitch's life even as we move forward with our own.

Exploring my spirituality after Mitch's death has also helped me heal. My faith has changed and deepened since Mitch died. At first I was furious with God, but by exploring my spirituality through discussions with spiritual leaders and friends, and after reading many books, I've found hope.

Even though Mitch is no longer here, I know he's not gone, either.

I encourage you to try some of the excellent ideas in this compassionate book. Learn more about grief and mourning. Find people who will listen to you tell your story of love and loss for your sibling. Become an advocate for yourself and your own healing—especially in our culture, which tends to downplay the importance of sibling loss.

You miss your brother or sister. I deeply miss Mitch, too. We understand each other, you and I. I hope you will be comforted in the knowledge that others have walked the same path you walk and have ultimately found a sense of peace.

Amy Anderson

INTRODUCTION

"To the outside world we all grow old. But not to brothers and sisters. We know each other as we always were. We know each other's hearts. We share private family jokes. We remember family feuds and secrets, family griefs and joys. We live outside the touch of time."

—Clara Ortega

Your brother or sister has died. I am truly sorry for your loss.

Whether your sibling was younger or older, whether the death was sudden or anticipated, whether you were very close to your sibling throughout your lives or experienced periods of separation, you are now grieving.

To grieve is to experience thoughts and feelings of loss inside you. If you loved your sibling, you will grieve. Even if you had a difficult or ambivalent relationship with your sibling, you will grieve. The purpose of this book is to provide you with comfort and support as you express your grief, which is to mourn. And to mourn is to heal.

Sibling relationships

Brothers and sisters often have strong and ambivalent feelings for one another. Relationships among siblings tend to be very complex, characterized by a mixture of anger, jealousy, and a fierce closeness and love. What was your relationship with the sibling who died? I'll bet it wasn't entirely simple.

The reason that sibling relationships are so complex is that while we are growing up, siblings are both friends and enemies, teammates and competitors. We play with our siblings and we fight with our siblings. We share our parents' love and we compete for our parents' love. We enjoy being part of a family and we struggle to be seen as individuals. And as teenagers, we are developmentally tasked with separating from our families—casting our sibling relationships in a new light.

Sometimes we carry our childhood rivalries and differences into adulthood, and our ambivalent feelings toward our brothers and sisters remain. Sometimes we separate from our siblings completely as adults. And sometimes we become very close friends with our grown-up brothers and sisters.

Yet no matter what your present-day relationship with your sibling was, his or her death is a blow because a part of your story has died. You shared a history with your sibling. Your stories began together and were intimately intertwined for years. Who else knew you so well?

At any given time, an estimated 25 percent of Americans have experienced the death of a sibling. This means that nearly 100 million people in our country have suffered the death of a brother or sister. Yet why do we hear so little about sibling grief?

Disenfranchised grief

The loss of an adult sibling is often a significant one. I have had the privilege of companioning many mourners who have experienced the death of a sibling, and they have taught me that they often feel deep pain and a profound sense of loss. Perhaps this resonates with you and your experience.

Yet too often, our society views the death of an adult sibling as less important than the death of a spouse, a child, a parent, or even a close friend. This results in surviving siblings feeling unvalidated and unsupported in their grief. We sometimes call this "disenfranchised grief," meaning that it is not acknowledged in our culture. I also use the term "forgotten mourners" to describe this problem. Has this happened to you?

The truth is, no losses are "less than." They are simply different. What's more, the stronger your attachment to someone who dies, the stronger your grief is likely to be—no matter the type of relationship (spouse, child, parent, sibling, friend, etc.). Also, when relationships are strained, difficult or have been cut off, we often experience natural complications because we mourn for what we wish could have been.

If you are feeling disenfranchised in your grief over the loss of your sibling, you can choose to get the support you need. First, talk to your spouse, your children and your best friends about your thoughts and feelings. Tell them that you are struggling and that you need their help. Many people are willing and able to be supportive if only they are made aware that support is needed.

Second, seek out others who have experienced the death of a sibling. You will probably find that they understand your grief and are willing to talk to you about theirs. Some of these people may even help form a support group that you can participate in.

And third, consider seeing a grief counselor if support among your friends and family is lacking. Many (though perhaps not all) grief counselors understand that adult sibling loss can be just as difficult as other types of loss, and their compassionate support during your grief journey can make all the difference.

How to use this book

As promised, this book contains 100 ideas to help support you as you mourn the loss of your brother or sister. Some of the ideas will teach you about the principles of grief and mourning. One of the most important ways to help yourself is to learn about the grief experience. The remainder of the 100 ideas offer practical, here-and-now, action-oriented suggestions for embracing your grief and practicing self-compassion. Each idea is followed by a brief explanation of how and why the idea might help you.

Some of the ideas will speak to your unique experience better than others. If you come to an idea that doesn't seem to fit you, simply ignore it and turn to another page.

You'll also notice that each of the 100 ideas offers a "carpe diem," when means "seize the day." My hope is that you not relegate this book to your shelves but instead keep it handy on your nightstand or desk. Pick it up often and turn to any page; the carpe diem suggestion might help you seize the day by giving you an exercise, action or thought to consider today, right now, right this minute.

I hope the ideas explored throughout the following pages bring you some solace and help you be self-compassionate. The word compassion literally means "with passion." So, self-compassion means caring for oneself with passion. This book is intended to help you be kind to yourself during this naturally difficult time.

In addition to this resource, I would suggest that readers visit the excellent website www.adultsiblinggrief.com. This lovely site features general information, a message board, chat rooms, and additional written resources focused specifically on the needs of surviving adult siblings.

My hope for you

When T.J. Wray experienced the death of her 43-year-old brother, she described her experience as follows:

> *The year my brother died, I forgot how to breathe, and no one seemed to notice. After all, it was only my brother; I should get over it.*

My hope is that this book helps you acknowledge that you don't "get over" the death of your brother or sister. Instead, you live with and are forever changed by this huge loss.

To be "bereaved" literally means "to be torn apart" and "to have special needs." When a sibling dies, it is like a deep hole implodes inside of you. It's as if the hole penetrates you and leaves you gasping for air. I have always said that we mourn significant losses from the inside out. In my experience, it is only when we are nurtured (inside and outside) that we discover the courage to mourn openly and honestly.

Remember—you are not alone, and you are not forgotten. No, your love does not end with the death of your brother or sister. You can and will carry your sibling with you into the future, always remembering your past and what he or she brought to the dance of your life. I hope we meet one day.

Alan D. Wolfelt

1.

UNDERSTAND THE DIFFERENCE BETWEEN GRIEF AND MOURNING

- Grief is what we think and feel on the inside when someone we love dies.

- Mourning is the outward expression of our grief.

- Everyone grieves when someone loved dies, but if we are to heal, we must also mourn.

- Many of the ideas in this book are intended to help you mourn the death of your brother or sister, to express your grief outside of yourself. Over time and with the support of others, to mourn is to heal.

- If some of your friends and family are not compassionately supporting your need to mourn, seek out the company of those who will.

CARPE DIEM

Ask yourself this: Have I been mourning my sibling's death, or have I restricted myself to grieving?

2.

BE COMPASSIONATE WITH YOURSELF

- The journey through grief is a long and difficult one. It is also a journey for which there is no preparation.

- Be compassionate with yourself as you encounter painful thoughts and feelings.

- Don't judge yourself or try to set a particular course for healing. There is no one way to grieve the death of a sibling. There is only what you think and feel and the expressing of those thoughts and feelings.

- Let your journey be what it is. And let yourself—your new, grieving self—be who you are.

CARPE DIEM

If you have the energy, take a walk today through a quiet area of town. Or better yet, get out of town and find a "safe place" in nature. Rest when you're tired and contemplate the ways in which you might take better care of yourself in the coming weeks and months.

3.

DON'T EXPECT YOURSELF TO MOURN OR HEAL IN A CERTAIN WAY OR IN A CERTAIN TIME

- Your unique grief journey will be shaped by many factors, including:
    - the nature of the relationship you had with the sibling who died
    - the age of the sibling who died
    - your age
    - the circumstances of the death
    - your family's coping and communication styles
    - your unique personality
    - your cultural background
    - your religious or spiritual beliefs
    - your gender
    - your support systems

- Because of these and other factors, no two deaths are ever mourned in precisely the same way.

- Don't have rigid expectations for your thoughts, feelings and behaviors. Instead, celebrate your uniqueness.

- A special note on age: Even if your sibling was elderly when he or she died, your feelings of loss may be profound. Some people think that death is just a normal part of life for older people, and that they accept death more easily than younger people. While this may be true in part, elderly people still feel the pain of loss. Love is ageless, thus grief is ageless.

CARPE DIEM

Start a grief journal today. Each night before you go to sleep, spend a few minutes writing about your thoughts and feelings about your sibling's death. As time passes, reread your journal entries and note how your grief is changing.

4.

ALLOW FOR NUMBNESS

- Feelings of shock, numbness and disbelief are nature's way of temporarily protecting us from the full reality of the death of someone loved. They help us survive our early grief. I often say, "Thank God for numbness and denial."

- We often think, "I will wake up and this will not have happened." Mourning can feel like being in a dream. The world feels distant, almost unreal—especially the lives of other people. The world turns, but you may not feel it. Time moves, but you may not experience it.

- Your emotions need time to catch up with what your mind has been told. This is true even when death has followed a long illness.

- Even after you have moved beyond these initial feelings, don't be surprised if they reemerge. Birthdays, holidays and anniversaries often trigger these normal and necessary feelings.

CARPE DIEM

If you're feeling numb, cancel any commitments that require concentration and decision-making. Allow yourself time to regroup.

5.

EXPECT TO HAVE A
MULTITUDE OF FEELINGS

- Mourners don't just feel sad. We may feel numb, angry, guilty, afraid, confused or even relieved. Sometimes these feelings follow each other within a short period of time, or they may occur simultaneously.

- As strange as some of these emotions may seem to you, they are normal and healthy.

- Allow yourself to feel whatever it is you are feeling without judging yourself.

- Talk about your feelings with someone who cares and can supportively listen.

CARPE DIEM

Which emotion has surprised you most since your sibling's death?
In your mind, single out this emotion for a moment and give it play.
Embrace it. Honor it. And affirm it by talking to someone else who
has journeyed through grief after the death of someone loved.

6.

BE AWARE THAT YOUR GRIEF AFFECTS YOUR BODY, HEART, SOCIAL SELF AND SPIRIT

- Grief is physically demanding. The body responds to the stress of the encounter and the immune system can weaken. You may be more susceptible to illness and physical discomforts. You may also feel lethargic or highly fatigued. You may not be sleeping well.

- The emotional toll of grief is complex and painful. Mourners often feel many different feelings, and those feelings can shift and blur over time.

- Bereavement naturally results in social discomfort. Friends and family often withdraw from mourners, leaving us isolated and unsupported.

- Mourners often ask ourselves, "Why are we here?" "Will my life have meaning now?" "Where is God in this?" Spiritual questions such as these are natural and necessary but also draining.

- Basically, your grief may affect every aspect of your life. Nothing may feel "normal" right now. If this is true for you, don't be alarmed. Just trust that in time, you will find peace and comfort again.

CARPE DIEM

If you've felt physically affected by your grief, see a doctor this week. Sometimes it's comforting to receive a clean bill of health.

7.

EMBRACE YOUR SPIRITUALITY

• Above all, grief is a journey of the soul. It demands you to consider why people live, why people die and what gives life meaning. These are the most spiritual questions we have language to form.

• Since your sibling has died, you've probably found yourself contemplating your own death. This is very common. After all, now that your sibling has died, your own mortality may seem more real.

• For many people, formal places of worship—churches, synagogues, mosques—offer a safe place and a ritualized process for discovering and embracing their spirituality. If you don't belong to a place of worship, perhaps now is a good time to join.

• For me, spending time alone in nature provides both the solitude and the beautiful evidence of God's existence that I need to nurture my soul.

• We grow, we learn; the spiritual path is a lifetime unfolding process. The death of your sibling often inspires this spiritual unfolding. Make the effort to embrace your spirituality and it will embrace you back by inspiring you with a sense of peace, hope and healing.

CARPE DIEM

Perhaps you have a friend who seems spiritually grounded.
Talk to this person about his beliefs and spiritual experiences.
Ask him how he learned to nurture his spirituality.

8.

TELL THE STORY, OVER AND OVER AGAIN IF NECESSARY

- Acknowledging a death is a painful, ongoing need that we meet in doses, over time. A vital part of healing in grief is often "telling the story" over and over again.

- The "story" relates the circumstances surrounding the death, reviewing the relationship, describing aspects of the personality of the sibling who died, and sharing memories, good and bad.

- It's as if each time we tell the story, it becomes a little more real. It also becomes a more integrated part of who we are.

- Find people who are willing to listen to you tell your story, over and over again if necessary, without judgment.

CARPE DIEM

Tell the story to someone today in the form of a letter. Perhaps you can write and send this letter to a friend who lives far away. If you are not a letter writer, find a trusted friend to "talk out" the story. You will know who will be willing to listen and who won't.

9.

HELP ERADICATE THE MYTH THAT PEOPLE DON'T NEED TO MOURN WHEN AN ADULT SIBLING DIES

• Here's how the myth goes: When an adult dies, it is the parents, spouse and children of the person who died who suffer the greatest loss. Siblings are affected less deeply.

• But the truth is that the strength of the attachment is a measure of the strength of the loss. While grief cannot and should not be quantified, we can say that the more deeply you feel connected to someone, the more difficult his or her death will likely be for you. And siblings—even when they have not spent much time together as adults—often have profoundly strong attachments to one another.

• Also, be aware that you are at risk for having people minimize your need to mourn if you have had a strained, difficult or cut-off relationship with your sibling. Yet, sometimes you mourn for the relationship you wish you could have had with your brother or sister.

• Whether your sibling was young, middle-aged or older, whether the death was sudden or anticipated, someone you loved and who loved you will never be physically present to you again. Of course you grieve! Of course you need to mourn!

• When the opportunity arises, let others know that the death of a sibling is not easy and that the resulting grief is not "less than" the grief from other deaths.

CARPE DIEM

If you have a friend whose sibling has died, talk about this experience. Ask: What was it like for you when your brother or sister died? She may welcome the opportunity to express her thoughts and feelings, and you may be comforted by the knowledge that you're not alone.

10.

MOVE TOWARD YOUR GRIEF, NOT AWAY FROM IT

- Our society teaches us that emotional pain is to be avoided, not embraced, yet it is only in moving toward our grief that we can be healed.

- As Helen Keller once said, "The only way to get to the other side is to go through the door."

- Note that the phrase "move toward your grief" invites you to take an active role in your healing. Don't think of yourself as a powerless victim or as helpless in the face of grief. Instead, empower yourself to "do something" with your grief—to mourn it, to express it outside yourself, to find ways to help yourself heal.

- Be suspicious if you find yourself thinking that you're "doing well" since the death. Sometimes "doing well" means you're avoiding your pain.

CARPE DIEM

Today, do something to confront and express your grief. Maybe it's time to tell someone close to you how you've really been feeling.

11.

REVIEW YOUR RELATIONSHIP
WITH THE SIBLING WHO DIED

- One way to mourn your sibling's death is to think through, write and talk about the relationship you had with him or her. Were you close to your sibling, whether as children and/or as adults? How did your relationship change as you grew older? What words would your sibling use to describe you? What words would you use to describe your sibling?

- Also think about your feelings for your brother or sister and why those feelings were most prominent. What was your sibling like? How did you respond to him or her? How did your sibling help shape who you became?

- What was your role in your family? Were you the "smart one" or the "funny one" or the "troublemaker" or the "peacemaker?" What was your sibling's role? How did your roles interface with each other?

- Ultimately, thinking through these kinds of questions and talking or writing about them may help you reconcile ambivalent feelings and old hurts. You may achieve a sense of peace and understanding about your sibling and the life the two of you lived side by side.

CARPE DIEM

On a large piece of paper, draw a timeline of your life. Write in significant events and dates. Also write in significant events and dates in the life of your sibling. How did your two lives connect? How did your life affect your sibling's and vice versa?

12.

ACKNOWLEDGE ALL THE LOSSES THIS DEATH HAS BROUGHT ABOUT

- When a sibling dies, you lose not only the physical presence of your sibling, but also a part of yourself—that part of you that was and is a brother or sister.

- One of the most difficult losses for grieving adult siblings can be the sense of loss of a shared history. Your brother or sister grew up in the same house with you, shared the same parents, attended the same school, climbed the same tree... Who else knew your childhood so well?

- If you have children, you may also mourn the aunt or uncle they will no longer have and the sense of Family with a capital F that your sibling brought to any gathering.

- Perhaps you lead a busy life and did not spend as much time with your sibling in recent years as you wish you would have. His or her death may leave you feeling that you have lost time you can now never recapture.

- Allowing yourself to acknowledge the many levels of loss the death has brought to your life will help you move forward in your grief journey.

CARPE DIEM

Name the things that you've lost or events you'll mourn in the future as a result of your sibling's death.

13.

ALLOW FOR FEELINGS OF UNFINISHED BUSINESS

• The death of a sibling often brings about feelings of unfinished business— things we never did, things we didn't get to say, things we wish we hadn't.

• Allow yourself to think and feel through these "if onlys" and "should haves." You may never be able to fully resolve these issues, but if you permit yourself to mourn them, you will be become reconciled to them.

• Is there something you wanted to say to your sibling but never did? Write her a letter that openly expresses your thoughts and feelings— but only when you're ready. Or, it may be more natural for you to "talk out" these things with a trusted friend or counselor.

• Talk with your spouse, remaining siblings, parents or friends about these feelings. If you have surviving siblings, they probably have similar feelings of their own. Sharing them with each other may help you reconcile them.

CARPE DIEM

Take this opportunity to tie up any loose ends you may have with someone who's still alive. Express your feelings and renew your relationship.

14.

REACH OUT TO OTHERS FOR HELP

- Perhaps the most compassionate thing you can do for yourself at this difficult time is to reach out for help from others.

- Think of it this way: Grieving may be the hardest work you have ever done. And hard work is less burdensome when others lend a hand. Life's greatest challenges—getting through school, raising children, pursuing a career—are in many ways team efforts. So it should be with mourning.

- Sharing your pain with others won't make it disappear, but it will, over time, make it more bearable. Sibling mourners have told me they find it particularly helpful to talk to others who have experienced the death of a sibling. From our common bond comes hope for our mutual healing.

- Reaching out for help also connects you to other people and strengthens the bonds of love that make life seem worth living again.

CARPE DIEM

Call a close friend who may have distanced himself from you since the death and tell him how much you need him right now. Suggest specific ways he can help.

15.

IDENTIFY THREE PEOPLE YOU CAN TURN TO ANYTIME YOU NEED A FRIEND

- You may have many people who care about you but few who are able to be good companions in grief.

- Identify three people whom you think can be there for you in the coming weeks and months.

- Don't assume that others will help. Even normally compassionate people sometimes find it hard to be present to others in grief.

- I find that after a death, you can usually divide the people you know into three groups. The neutral group won't harm you in your grief, nor will they generally be of much help. The harmful group will make you feel worse by what they say or do. And the helpful group will be available to you and supportive of your need to mourn. Try to spend time with those who help, and set boundaries with those who are harmful to you right now.

CARPE DIEM

Call the three friends you've identified and ask them outright:
Are you willing to help me with my grief? Tell them you mainly
need to spend time with them and talk to them freely.

16.

UNDERSTAND THE SIX
NEEDS OF MOURNING

Need #1: Acknowledge the reality of the death.

- This first need of mourning requires you to gently confront the difficult reality that your sibling is dead and will never physically be present to you again.

- Whether the death was sudden or anticipated, acknowledging the full reality of the loss may occur over weeks and months.

- You will first acknowledge the reality of the loss with your head. Only over time will you come to acknowledge it with your heart.

- At times you may push away the reality of your sibling's death. This is normal. You will come to integrate the reality, in doses, as you are ready.

CARPE DIEM

Tell someone about the death today. You might talk about the circumstances of the death or review the relationship you had with your sister or brother. Talking about it will help you work on this important need.

17.

UNDERSTAND THE SIX NEEDS OF MOURNING

Need #2: Embrace the pain of the loss.

- This need requires mourners to embrace the pain of their loss—something we naturally don't want to do. It is easier to avoid, repress or push away the pain of grief than it is to confront it.

- It is in embracing your grief, however, that you will learn to reconcile yourself to it.

- Always remember that your pain is normal and necessary. You are not being "overly emotional" if you feel devastated after the death of a sibling. You are not being irrational. You are not weak or immature. The bond between siblings can run very deep, and its history tells, in large part, the story of who you are.

- You will probably need to "dose" yourself in embracing your pain. If you were to allow in all the pain at once, you would not survive.

CARPE DIEM

If you feel up to it, allow yourself a time for embracing pain today. Dedicate 15 minutes to thinking about and feeling the loss. Reach out to someone who doesn't try to take your pain away and spend some time with him.

18.

UNDERSTAND THE SIX
NEEDS OF MOURNING

Need #3: Remember the sibling who died.

- When someone loved dies, they live on in us through memory.

- To heal, you need to actively remember the sibling who died and commemorate the life that was lived.

- Never let anyone take your memories away in a misguided attempt to save you from pain. It's good for you to continue to display photos of your brother or sister. It's good for you to talk about your sibling's life and death. It's good for you to hold onto objects that belonged to your sibling.

- Remembering the past makes hoping for the future possible. As E.M. Forster wrote, "Unless we remember, we cannot understand." And, as Kierkegaard noted, "Life is lived forward but understood backward."

CARPE DIEM

Brainstorm a list of characteristics or memories of your sibling. Write as fast as you can for 10 minutes (or more), then put away your list for later reflection.

19.

UNDERSTAND THE SIX
NEEDS OF MOURNING

Need #4: Develop a new self-identity.

- A large part of your self-identity was formed by the relationship you had with the sibling who died. For all (or most) of your life, you have been the brother or sister of the sibling who died. You have been a member of your family of origin.

- A hole has been made in your identity. If your only sibling died, you may feel like an "only child." Do you still have a surviving brother or sister? If so, how will you answer the common, casual question: "How many brothers and sisters do you have?" The way you defined yourself and the way society defines you is changed.

- You need to re-anchor yourself, to reconstruct your self-identity. This is arduous and painful work.

- Many mourners discover that as they work on this need, they ultimately discover some positive changes, such as becoming more caring or less judgmental.

CARPE DIEM

Write out a response to this prompt: I used to be _____.
Now that _____ died, I am _____. This makes me
feel _____. Keep writing as long as you want.

20.

UNDERSTAND THE SIX NEEDS OF MOURNING

Need #5: Search for meaning.

- When someone we love dies, we naturally question the meaning and purpose of life and death.

- "Why?" questions may surface uncontrollably and often precede "How" questions. Questions such as "Why did my brother die this way?" or "Why did my sister have to get sick?" often come before "How will I go on living?"

- You will probably question your philosophy of life and explore religious and spiritual values as you work on this need.

- Remember that having faith or spirituality does not negate your need to mourn. Even if you believe in life after death or that your sibling has gone to "a better place," you still have the right and the need to mourn this significant loss in your life. "Blessed are those who mourn for they shall be comforted."

CARPE DIEM

Write down a list of "why" questions that may have surfaced for you since the death. Find a friend or counselor who will explore these questions with you without thinking she has to give you answers.

21.

UNDERSTAND THE SIX
NEEDS OF MOURNING

Need #6: Receive ongoing support from others.

- As mourners, we need the love and understanding of others if we are to heal.

- If you feel dependent on others right now, don't feel ashamed. Instead, revel in the knowledge that others care about you. Acknowledging your need for support is not a weakness, it is a strength.

- Unfortunately, our society places too much value on "carrying on" and "doing well" after a death. Grieving siblings are especially forgotten. So, many grieving siblings are abandoned by their friends and family soon after the death.

- Grief is a process, not an event, and you will need the continued support of your friends and family for weeks, months and years.

CARPE DIEM

Sometimes your friends want to support you but don't know
how. Ask. Call your closest friend right now and tell her you
need her help through the coming weeks and months.

22.

KNOW THAT GRIEF DOES NOT PROCEED IN ORDERLY, PREDICTABLE "STAGES"

- Though the "Needs of Mourning" (Ideas 16-21) are numbered 1-6, grief is not an orderly progression towards healing. Don't fall into the trap of thinking your grief journey will be predictable or always forward-moving.

- Usually, grief hurts more before it hurts less.

- You will probably experience a multitude of different emotions in a wave-like fashion. You will also likely encounter more than one need of mourning at the same time.

- Be compassionate with yourself as you experience your own unique grief journey.

CARPE DIEM

Has anyone told you that you are in this or that "stage" of grief? Ignore this usually well-intended advice. Don't allow yourself or anyone else to compartmentalize your grief.

23.

IF YOU STILL HAVE LIVING BROTHERS OR SISTERS, CONSIDER THIS

- The death of a sibling seems always to be a shock, whether the death was sudden or anticipated. Your sibling was and always will be one of the central figures in your life. Even siblings who aren't seemingly close play a large psychological and emotional role in our lives.

- If your sibling was the first significant person in your life to die, you may find yourself encountering grief and the harsh realities of death for the first time. This is never easy.

- What do siblings represent? They are mirrors of our history and childhood; they are connections to the past; they are journeyers on parallel paths; they are affirmers of our very existence. When a sibling dies, all of these things are torn at the seams.

- Now that one of your siblings has died, perhaps you can use your newfound perspective to strengthen your relationship with your surviving siblings. How much time might you have left together?

CARPE DIEM

Choose a gift for a surviving sibling, parent or family member today. Try to find something emotionally resonant—not necessarily expensive or practical. Wrap it with care and include a note telling him how you feel about him. Bring or ship him the gift as soon as possible.

24.

BE COMPASSIONATE WITH OTHERS WHO MOURN THIS DEATH

- Of course, you are not alone in mourning this death. If your parents are still alive, they will be profoundly affected. If your sibling had a life partner and/or children, they will obviously need support as well. Friends and neighbors are probably grieving too.

- While you should not subordinate your grief to that of other family members—remember, sibling grief is not less important!—you *can* be a catalyst for healing in your family. Reaching out to others who mourn this death will help you and them.

- Compassion means "with passion"—with feeling and empathy. Self-compassion, then, is having empathy towards oneself. Be compassionate towards others and self-compassionate to yourself in the difficult weeks and months to come.

CARPE DIEM

Write, call or visit a surviving family member today. For this one day, concentrate on practicing active empathy—understanding your family member's grief experience from his or her perspective.

25.

LOOK TO THOSE WHO MODEL HOPE AND HEALING

- As we have said, you are not alone. While no one else feels and grieves exactly as you do over the death of this one special person, many others have experienced similar deaths and learned to live and love fully again.

- You may find it helpful to identify people who have not only survived the death of an adult sibling but who have learned to live more deeply as a result.

- Grief support groups may put you in touch with such people. You can also find many good books written by grieving adult siblings. (Visit amazon.com and search "adult sibling grief." There are a number of excellent books out there!)

- Your place of worship may offer opportunities for you to meet others affected by adult sibling loss. You may want to look into support groups, lay ministries and weekend retreats.

CARPE DIEM

Whom do you know who—despite adversity—exhibits the kind of love and hopefulness you'd like to regain? Contact this person and ask for his advice over lunch or coffee.

26.

IF YOU FIND YOURSELF "SEARCHING" FOR YOUR SIBLING, KNOW THAT THIS IS NORMAL

- When someone loved dies, we often "search" for them—knowingly or unknowingly.

- You may find yourself driving past your sibling's house, expecting an e-mail from him or her, following cars that look like your sibling's, hearing his voice in a crowded restaurant.

- These searching behaviors are normal. Your mind is simply trying to find evidence that will disprove a truth it doesn't want to believe.

- At times, you may sense that your sibling is near. I hope you choose to be comforted by this feeling.

CARPE DIEM

The next time you find yourself searching for your sibling, write the experience down. If you record your searching behaviors, you may learn something about yourself and your journey to healing.

27.

BRACE YOURSELF FOR THE WORDS

- They're such simple, everyday words: "brother" and "sister." Yet now, whenever you hear them, you may feel deep pain.

- Now that you've become sensitized to these words, you'll probably hear them often.

- In the weeks and months to come, you will probably come to some understanding within yourself about the quality of your ongoing sisterhood or brotherhood with the sibling who died.

- Maybe it will help you to say a silent "I love you and I miss you" every time you hear these words.

CARPE DIEM

Keep track of how many times you hear the words brother and sister this week. Put a quarter in a jar for each time. Keep doing this and pretty soon you'll have enough money to buy something special.

28.

IF YOUR SIBLING DIED AFTER AN EXTENDED ILLNESS OR DECLINE, KNOW THAT FEELINGS OF RELIEF ARE PERFECTLY NORMAL

- If your brother or sister died after an extended illness or decline, what you may feel above all else is a tremendous sense of relief. If you cared for or spent time with your sibling while he suffered, you may even have wished—prayed!—for a swift death.

- Feelings of relief after a prolonged or painful illness is ended by death are very common. It is perfectly normal and understandable to want your sibling's suffering to end and your life to return to normal.

- Of course, you've probably found that your life is not "normal" anymore. Your sibling has died. Your life is forever changed. And even though you were anticipating the death, you may still feel shocked when it actually happens. No one is ever really prepared for the death of someone loved.

- If the death was recent, you may be worried if all you can seem to remember or think about is your sibling's suffering and death. Rest assured that in time, you will once again recall happier, gentler memories.

CARPE DIEM

Call or write a note to someone else who was involved in your sibling's care during the last days or weeks. Share your feelings with this person and thank her for her concern and help.

29.

ALLOW YOURSELF TO BE
SELF-ABSORBED

- If you are feeling self-absorbed since the death, caught up in your own thoughts and feelings, good for you.

- Your thoughts and feelings need your attention right now. YOU need your attention right now.

- If you're unable to attend to the needs of others right now, that's OK. If you need help looking after your kids for a bit, find someone to help.

- You're not selfish, you're grieving. You have special needs that demand a great deal of energy right now.

CARPE DIEM

If someone is angry or annoyed with you about your apparent disregard for others right now, talk to him or her. Explain that your grief is making you turn inward and that you need this time to heal.

30.

IF YOUR SIBLING DIED SUDDENLY, LOOK FOR WAYS TO EMBRACE THE REALITY OF THE DEATH

- The sudden death of a sibling, like any sudden death, comes as a shock. For a while, the death may seem completely unreal and dreamlike. You may feel as if your brother or sister will phone or walk through your door at any moment.

- This heightened sense of disbelief protects you in the early days and weeks after the death. If your mind were to force you to confront the reality all at once, you could not survive.

- But later, as you are ready, confronting the reality of the death in doses will help you heal. Encourage yourself to talk about the death. Look at photos of the sibling who died. Visit the place of the death and/or your sibling's home. Talk with the last people to speak with your sibling.

- Embracing the reality of the death can be painful, but even more painful in the long run is pushing it away. To come to terms with this sudden death is to come to terms with continued life.

CARPE DIEM

If the death was sudden, close your eyes and imagine your sibling's last days or hours. What was she doing when she died? What was the weather like? What were you doing? What thoughts or words would you have conveyed to her at that moment if you could have?

31.

IF YOUR RELATIONSHIP WITH YOUR SIBLING WAS STRAINED OR NONEXISTENT, ALLOW FOR AMBIVALENT FEELINGS

- Sometimes adult siblings grow apart and rarely, if ever, speak to one another. At times this separation is a result of longstanding differences in values, personality and lifestyle. At other times, this phenomenon simply results from the fact that we lead busy—and separate—lives, especially when we live far apart.

- If you and your sibling rarely communicated with one another, you may still feel a surprisingly deep sense of loss. After all, someone with whom you once shared a family and a home is now gone forever. It is too late to reconnect. You may struggle with feelings of guilt and regret. You may not have realized until now that your sibling was still an important part of your heart.

- If your relationship with your sibling was strained due to differences in values, personality or lifestyle, you may feel a mixture of feelings after her death. You may feel angry about the choices she made.

- Sometimes you may secretly feel that the "wrong" sibling has died. Perhaps the sibling you were closer to has died, or the younger sibling or the one who seemed in better health. These feelings are normal and do not indicate a lack of love or compassion, though you may want to explore them further by journaling them or discussing them with someone you trust.

CARPE DIEM

Such ambivalent feelings are normal and natural. Explore them by talking with others who cared about your sibling.

32.

ACCEPT DIFFERENT GRIEF RESPONSES AMONG FAMILY MEMBERS

- Just as there is no one right way for you to mourn, there is no one right way for other family members to mourn. You are likely to find that each of you will mourn the death in markedly different ways.

- The building block of our life is our own singularity. Even when we are kin, we are all individually stamped. Our personalities are as unique as fingerprints.

- If you have surviving siblings, you will find that each of them will mourn this death in his or her own way. While you might have anticipated some of your siblings' responses since the death (for example, your emotional sister has probably been emotional), other responses may have surprised you. Try not to let these differences alarm you or hurt your feelings.

- If your parents are still alive, they, too, will have their own unique responses to the death. You can help by facilitating open and honest communication with them about their grief and yours.

- If your sibling had a spouse and children, their grief responses will also be highly individual.

- Feelings will naturally run high in your family in the weeks and months after the death. The best approach is to be open with one another without blaming.

CARPE DIEM

If you haven't talked to a certain family member recently, call him today. Tell him you've been thinking about him. Ask him how he's been doing since your sibling's death. Ask him how his life has changed. You might be surprised by his answers.

33.

LIVE IN THE MOMENT

- Grief is a one-day-at-a-time journey, and some days are better than others.

- Actually, grief is a one-moment-at-a-time journey. What are you thinking and feeling this very second?

- If you try, you can teach your mind to attune to the physical sensations of the moment—the sound of the crickets chirping, the feeling of the breeze in your hair, the faces of those you love who are still present to you.

- Getting better at living in the now will help you appreciate your life today. This is not to take away your right and your need to mourn, but it is a way to blend living fully with mourning.

CARPE DIEM

Close your eyes right now. What do you hear? Breathe deeply and attend to the sound of your breath…in, out…in, out…in, out.

34.

NURTURE YOUR RELATIONSHIPS WITH YOUR SPOUSE AND CHILDREN

- Times of illness and death are stressful for everyone involved. Your sibling's death—and your reaction to it—has affected many people, including your spouse and your children.

- Have you been open with your partner and children about the effect this death has had on you? Have you communicated your grief? Have you talked to them about theirs?

- If your family hasn't been doing such a good job of openly mourning this death, it's not too late to start. Arrange some quiet time with your spouse and tell him how you've been feeling. Schedule a family meeting and ask everyone to share their feelings about the death.

- You've probably learned many things from your sibling's death—what it means to love your family, what's truly important to you, how life should be lived. Now's the time to translate these lessons into action.

CARPE DIEM

Today, surprise your partner with flowers or a small gift.
Tell her how much you love her and how grateful you were
to have her by your side when your sibling died.

35.

IF YOU ARE ANGRY, FIND APPROPRIATE WAYS TO EXPRESS YOUR ANGER

- For some people who are grieving the death of an adult sibling, feelings of shock and disbelief after the death are followed by anger.

- You may be angry at medical caregivers, your parents, your family, your spouse, even the sibling who died.

- Maybe you believe one of your family members is behaving inappropriately since the death. Maybe the death resulted from an accident that you believe could have been prevented. Maybe your spouse has been unsupportive.

- Feelings of anger at the sibling who died are quite common. Perhaps you're angry that he didn't quit smoking or didn't see the doctor sooner. Or maybe he left behind a financial or legal mess that his family now has to clean up.

- Anger is normal and necessary. It's our way of protesting a reality we don't like. It helps us survive. And anger is far sounder than a resignation to despair. Anger and feelings of protest challenge relationships, where despair severs or cuts off relationships. Anger may be frightening, but indifference is deadening.

CARPE DIEM

Today, do something physical to vent your anger. Go for a fast walk or punch a boxing bag. Smash a tennis ball against a practice wall over and over.

36.

IF YOU ARE UPSET ABOUT THE MEDICAL CARE YOUR SIBLING RECEIVED, EXPRESS THOSE FEELINGS

- The modern medical system can be exasperating for patients and their families. If your sibling was ill before she died, she may have endured countless doctor visits, tests, diagnoses and treatments.

- But in the end, modern medicine was not able to "cure" your sibling. You may feel frustrated that the treatments didn't work. You may feel angry at busy doctors, who perhaps seemed brusque or unthorough. You may feel bad decisions were made. You may feel your sibling suffered too much or too long.

- If you harbor bad feelings about your sibling's medical care, find a way to express those feelings. I'm not talking about frivolous lawsuits here. I'm simply suggesting that talking out your grievances about your sibling's medical care may help you move beyond them to the real work of mourning the death itself.

- Write a letter to the doctor or practice or hospital expressing your concerns, even if you never send it. Do you personally know someone in the medical field? Talk to this person about your feelings; he may be able to provide some "inside" perspective. Or talk out your feelings with your family.

CARPE DIEM

While you may feel upset about some aspect of your sibling's care, you probably feel grateful about another. Write a note of thanks to a caregiver who was particularly compassionate or helpful.

37.

IF YOU ARE A TWIN, SEEK EXTRA SUPPORT

- Twins typically have very close relationships.

- Studies show that even twins who were separated at birth and grew up in different families often have remarkably similar values and habits.

- If you are a twin whose twin brother or sister has died, you may be especially devastated by this death. Twins often report a sense of being halved after their twin has died. Without their twin, they simply do not feel whole.

- Your grief work may be particularly arduous. I recommend that you seek the support of an experienced grief counselor if you are struggling. The wonderful website www.twinlesstwins.org and the resources this organization offers may also be of help.

CARPE DIEM

If you know other twins, contact them today and make arrangements to get together. Their unique understanding may help you through this difficult time.

38.

EMBRACE THE HEALING POWER OF LINKING OBJECTS

- Linking objects are items that belonged to or remind you of the sibling who died.

- Photographs, videos, CDs, ticket stubs, clothing, gifts you received from him or her—all of these may now serve as reminders of your loss.

- Some items may bring sadness, some happiness, some sappiness (i.e., this is when you are happy and sad at the same time).

- While linking objects may evoke painful feelings, they are healing feelings. They help you embrace the pain of your loss (see idea 17) and move toward reconciliation.

- Whatever you do, DO NOT get rid of linking objects that remind you of the sibling who died. If you need to box some of them up for a time, do so. Later, when you are ready, you will likely find that displaying linking objects in your home is a way to remember the sibling who died and honor your ongoing feelings of love and loss.

CARPE DIEM

Look into obtaining a special object or two from your sibling's home. It may be a photo, a jacket, a pennant, a piece of jewelry—something you can cherish and keep close to you in the months and years to come.

39.

RELEASE ANY BAD FEELINGS OR REGRETS YOU MAY HAVE ABOUT THE FUNERAL AND BURIAL

- The funeral is a wonderful means of expressing our beliefs, thoughts and feelings about the death of someone loved. I hope you had a meaningful funeral service in honor of your brother or sister.

- Funerals help us acknowledge the reality of the death, give testimony to the life of the person who died, express our grief, support each other and embrace our faith and beliefs about life and death.

- Yet for many mourners, funeral planning is difficult. Funeral and burial decisions may have been made quickly, while you were still in deep shock and disbelief. Sometimes some of these decisions seem wrong with the benefit of hindsight.

- If you harbor any negative feelings about your sibling's funeral or memorial service, know this: You and everyone else who was a part of the service did the best they could do at the time. You cannot change what happened, but you can talk about what happened and share your thoughts and feelings with someone who cares. Don't berate yourself.

- It's never too late to hold another memorial service for your sibling. Perhaps a tree-planting ceremony or a small gathering on the anniversary of the sibling's death could be a forum for sharing memories and prayer. Ask a clergyperson or someone you know to be a good public speaker to help plan and lead the ceremony.

CARPE DIEM

If you harbor regrets or anger about your sibling's funeral and burial, talk about these feelings with someone today. Perhaps the two of you together can create an "action plan" to help make things better.

40.

GO TO EXILE

- Choosing to spend time alone is an essential self-nurturing spiritual practice. Alone time affords you the opportunity to be unaffected by others' wants and needs. Solitude is a requirement if you are going to honor that you mourn from the inside out.

- It is impossible to really know yourself if you never take time to withdraw from the demands of daily living. Alone time does not mean you are being selfish. Instead, you will experience rest and renewal in ways you otherwise would not.

- Getting away from it all can become your refuge. So much of modern life invites you to keep busy and stay active—email, cell phones, satellite TV—all competing for your attention. Yet, when you have special mourning needs, the last thing you need is all of these distractions.

- Even Jesus went to exile. He modeled the simple spiritual practice of rest and alone time as a natural , nourishing, and valuable counterpoint to times of busyness. Jesus would sometimes send people away, disappear without warning or explanation, and retreat to a place of rest. I guess if Jesus went to exile, so can you!

- Within your exiled time and space evolve the insights and blessings that come to the surface only in stillness and with time. Schedule alone time on a regular basis. Don't shut out your family and friends altogether, but do answer the call for contemplative alone time.

CARPE DIEM

Schedule one hour of solitude into your day today.

41.

CRY

- Tears are a natural cleansing and healing mechanism. It's OK to cry. In fact, it's good to cry when you feel like it. What's more, tears are a form of mourning. They are sacred!

- On the other hand, don't feel bad if you aren't crying a lot. Not everyone is a crier.

- You may find that those around you are uncomfortable with your tears. As a society, we're often not so good at witnessing others in pain.

- Explain to your friends and family that you need to cry right now and that they can help by allowing you to.

- You may find yourself crying at unexpected times or places. If you need to, excuse yourself and retreat to somewhere private. But don't feel shame; you are entitled to your tears.

CARPE DIEM

If you feel like it, have a good cry today. Find a safe place to embrace your pain and cry as long and as hard as you want to.

42.

REACH OUT AND TOUCH

- For many people, physical contact with another human being is healing. It has been recognized since ancient times as having transformative, healing powers.

- Have you hugged anyone lately? Held someone's hand? Put your arm around another human being?

- You probably know several people who enjoy hugging or physical touching. If you're comfortable with their touch, encourage it in the weeks and months to come.

- Hug someone you feel safe with. Get a full-body massage. Kiss your children or a friend's baby. Walk arm in arm with a neighbor.

CARPE DIEM

Try hugging your close friends and family members today,
even if you usually don't. You just might like it!

43.

WRITE A LETTER

- Sometimes articulating our thoughts and feelings in letter form helps us understand them better.

- Write a letter to your sibling telling him or her how you feel now. Consider the following prompts:
    - What I miss most about you is . . .
    - What I wish I'd said or hadn't said is . . .
    - What I remember best about you when we were growing up is…
    - What's hardest for me now is . . .
    - What I'd like to ask you is . . .
    - I'm keeping my memories of you alive by . . .

- Read your letter aloud at the cemetery or to a trusted friend.

- Write a letter to God telling him how you feel about the death.

- Write thank you notes to helpers such as hospice staff, neighbors, doctors, funeral directors, etc.

CARPE DIEM

Write a letter to someone you love who's still alive telling her why she's so important to you. Such letters become treasured keepsakes.

44.

BE MINDFUL OF ANNIVERSARIES

- Anniversaries—of the death, life events, birthdays—can be especially hard when you are in grief.

- These are times you may want to plan ahead for. Perhaps you could take a day off work on the anniversary of the death. Maybe on the next birthday of the sibling who died you could visit the cemetery or scattering site.

- Reach out to others on these difficult days. Talk about your feelings with a close friend.

CARPE DIEM

What's the next anniversary you're anticipating? Make a plan right now for what you will do on that day. Enlist a friend's help so you won't be alone.

45.

TAKE GOOD CARE OF YOURSELF

- Good self-care is nurturing and necessary for mourners, yet it's something many of us completely overlook.

- Try very hard to eat well and get adequate rest. Lay your body down 2-3 times a day for 20-30 minutes, even if you don't sleep. I know— you probably don't care very much about eating well right now, and you may be sleeping poorly. But taking care of yourself is truly one way to fuel healing and to begin to embrace life again.

- Drink at least 5-6 glasses of water each day. Dehydration can compound feelings of fatigue and disorientation.

- Exercise not only provides you with more energy, it can give you focused thinking time. Take a 20-minute walk every day. Or, if that seems too much, a 5-minute walk. But don't over-exercise, because your body needs extra rest, as well.

- Now more than ever, you need to allow time for you.

CARPE DIEM

Are you taking a multi-vitamin? If not, now
is probably a good time to start.

46.

IF YOU FEEL GUILTY, EXPLORE YOUR FEELINGS OF GUILT

- Some surviving siblings feel, among other things, guilt that they survived and their sibling did not.

- Would you have changed places with your sibling if you could have? Many surviving brothers and sisters feel this way. Others do not. Both are perfectly normal and natural responses.

- Life is unfair—and random. The fact that you are alive and your sibling is not may make no rational sense.

- You may also feel guilty that you didn't visit your sibling, that your life is more comfortable than hers was, that you never apologized for something you did wrong.

- No matter the source of your feelings of guilt, they are normal and natural. Allowing yourself to explore them will help you come to terms with them.

CARPE DIEM

Talk to someone today about your guilty feelings, however irrational you may know they are. Tell this person that you don't need him or her to absolve you of your guilt—you just need an empathetic listener.

47.

KEEP A JOURNAL

- Journals are an ideal way for some mourners to record thoughts and feeling.

- Remember—your inner thoughts and feelings about the death of your sibling need to be expressed outwardly (which includes writing) if you are to heal.

- Consider jotting down your thoughts and feelings each night before you go to sleep. Your journal entries can be as long or as short as you want. Don't worry about your vocabulary, sentence structure, punctuation, etc. The important thing is to express what's going on inside.

- Or keep a dream journal, instead. Keep a blank book in your nightstand for recording your dreams when you wake up.

- If you're not a writer, consider talking your thoughts and feelings into a tape recorder. Your audio journal might allow you to say things you otherwise might not say. And replaying your journal entries in the months and years that follow might help you recognize your progress and growth.

CARPE DIEM

Stop by your local bookstore and choose a blank book you like the look and feel of. Visit a park on your way home and write your first entry.

48.

ORGANIZE A TREE PLANTING

- Trees represent the beauty, vibrancy and continuity of life.

- A specially planted and located tree can honor your sibling and serves as a perennial memorial.

- You might write a short ceremony for the tree planting. (Or ask another family member to write one.) Consider a personalized metal marker or sign, too.

- For a more private option, plant a tree in your own yard. Consult your local nursery for an appropriate selection. Flowering trees are especially beautiful in the spring. You might also consider a variety of tree that your sibling loved or that reminds you of the family home in which you and your sibling grew up.

CARPE DIEM

Order a tree for your own yard and plant it in honor of
the sibling who died. You'll probably need someone
to help you prepare the hole and place the tree.

49.

PLAN A CEREMONY

- When words are inadequate, have ceremony.

- Ceremony assists in reality, recall, support, expression, transcendence.

- When personalized, the funeral ceremony can be a healing ritual. But ceremonies that take place later on can also be very meaningful.

- The ceremony might center on memories of your sibling, "meaning of life" thoughts and feelings or affirmation of faith.

- Our culture doesn't always understand the value of ceremony. Don't expect that everyone around you will understand your desire to make use of ritual. However, don't allow their lack of understanding to persuade you to forego ceremonies both at the time of the death and months and years into the future.

CARPE DIEM

Hold a candle-lighting memory ceremony. Invite a small group of friends. Form a circle around a center candle, with each person holding their own small candle. Have each person light their memory candle and share a special memory of your brother or sister. At the end, play a song or read a poem or prayer in memory of the sibling who died.

50.

ORGANIZE A MEMORY BOOK

- Assembling a scrapbook that holds treasured photos and mementos of your sibling can be a very healing activity.

- You might consider including a copy of her birth certificate, photographs, newspaper clippings, locks of hair, old letters—anything that helps capture the life of your sibling or seems meaningful to you.

- Phone others who loved your sibling and ask them to write a note or contribute photos.

- You could also write a storybook about growing up with your sibling. Is there a particular memory or incident that would make a good children's book?

- Other ideas: a memory box, a memory quilt, a personalized website. Find a seamstress who can turn an old shirt or blouse of your sibling's into a stuffed animal. These can make wonderful "linking objects," even for us grown-ups!

CARPE DIEM

Buy an appropriate scrapbook or keepsake box today. Don't forget to buy the associated materials you'll need, such as photo pages or photo corners, glue, scissors, etc.

51.

SHARE THE BURDEN

- If your sibling's death has generated additional tasks or to-dos for survivors, share the burden.

- Don't be a martyr and take on tasks that will overwhelm you. If you are taking care of mountains of paperwork or cleaning out your sibling's apartment, ask for help.

- Alternately, if your sibling's spouse and children need day-to-day, practical help right now, perhaps you could offer to pick up some of the slack.

- When people come together to support one another, grace happens.

CARPE DIEM

If it's needed, help plan a family workday to complete
a task that your sibling left unfinished.

52.

FIND A PLACE FOR YOUR LOVE

- Part of the grief journey involves figuring out what to do with the feelings of love you still have for your brother or sister.

- When your sibling was still present to you physically, your love emanated from you and flowed into him or her. You expressed your love through your words, your touch, your body language, and your deeds. And you knew that your love was received.

- What do you do with those feelings of love now, when there is no person to talk to, to touch, to smile at?

- While you cannot replace your sibling, you can find ways to express your ongoing love. You might find it helpful to talk to him or her—aloud or in your mind—when you have something to say. You might share your thoughts and feelings with someone who will listen. Or you might channel your love into caring for others. (However, be certain not to try to care for others right away. In the face of loss, you must first receive before you can effectively give.)

CARPE DIEM

The next time you're missing your sibling, ask yourself: Who needs this love I'm feeling? Reach out to someone in need of your caring.

53.

DON'T BE CAUGHT OFF GUARD BY "GRIEFBURSTS"

• Sometimes heightened periods of sadness overwhelm mourners. These times can seem to come of out nowhere and can be frightening and painful.

• Even long after the death, something as simple as a sound, a smell or a phrase that reminds you of your sibling can bring on a "griefburst."

• Allow yourself to experience griefbursts without shame or self-judgment, no matter where and when they occur. If you would feel more comfortable, retreat to somewhere private when these strong feelings surface.

CARPE DIEM

Create an action plan for your next griefburst. For example, you might plan to drop whatever you are doing and go for a walk or record thoughts in your journal.

54.

THINK YOUNG

- It is the nature of children to live for the moment and appreciate today. All of us would benefit from a little more childlike wonder.

- Do something childish—blow bubbles, skip rope, visit a toy store, build a sand castle, fly a kite, climb a tree.

- If kids aren't already a part of your life, make arrangements to spend some time with them. Volunteer at a local school. Take a friend's children to the park one afternoon.

- What special memories do you cherish from your childhood? Was there something you and your brother or sister liked to do together? Maybe you could do the same activity with your own children.

CARPE DIEM

Buy a gift for a child today just because.

55.

FOLLOW YOUR NOSE

- For centuries people have understood that certain smells induce certain feelings. Aromatherapy is the contemporary term for this age-old practice.

- Some comforting, memory-inducing smells include baby powder, freshly cut grass, dill, oranges, leather, lilacs.

- Essential oils, available at your local drugstore or bath and body shop, can be added to bath water or dabbed lightly on pulse points.

- Lavender relaxes. Rosewood and bergamot together lift the spirits. Peppermint invigorates. Chamomile and lavender are sleep aids.

CARPE DIEM

Visit a local bath and body shop and choose one or two
essential oils or scented candles. Try using them today.

56.

LISTEN TO THE MUSIC

- Music can be very healing to mourners because it helps us access our feelings, both happy and sad. Music can soothe the spirit and nurture the heart.

- What kind of music did your brother or sister listen to? Listening to this music can help you remember and feel close to your sibling.

- All types of music can be healing—rock & roll, classical, blues, folk.

- Consider listening to music you normally don't, perhaps the opera or the symphony. Or make a recording of your favorite songs, all together on one play-list.

- Do you play an instrument or sing? Allow yourself the time to try these activities again soon.

CARPE DIEM

Visit a music store today—online or in person—and sample a few CDs. Buy yourself the music that moves you the most.

57.

PRAY

- Prayer is a way of communicating your innermost thoughts and feelings to the powers of the universe. As such, prayer is a form of mourning. And studies have shown that prayer can actually help people heal.

- If you believe in a higher power, pray. Pray for your sibling who died. Pray for your questions about life and death to be answered. Pray for the strength to embrace your pain and to heal over time. Pray for others affected by this death.

- When you were a child, you and your siblings may have had a simple prayer to say at bedtime. Do you remember it? Try adding it to your bedtime routine once again.

- Many places of worship have prayer lists. Call yours and ask that your name be added to the prayer list. On worship day, the whole congregation will pray for you. Often many individuals will pray at home for those on the prayer list, as well.

CARPE DIEM

Bow your head right now and say a silent prayer. If you are out of practice, don't worry; just let your thoughts flow naturally.

58.

LEARN SOMETHING NEW

- Sometimes mourners feel stuck. We can feel depressed and the daily routine of our lives can be joyless.

- Perhaps you would enjoy learning something new or trying a new hobby.

- What have you always wanted to learn but have never tried? Playing the guitar? Woodworking? Speaking French? Is there something your sibling always wanted to learn to do but never did? Maybe you could learn on her behalf.

- Consider physical activities. Learning to play golf or doing karate have the added benefits of exercise.

- Some people like to try a hobby or activity their brother or sister once enjoyed. This can be a way of giving tribute to your sibling and feeling close to her at the same time.

CARPE DIEM

Get a hold of your local community calendar and sign up
for a class in something you have never tried before.

59.

TAKE A RISK

- For some, activities that harbor risk, real or perceived, are invigorating and life-affirming.

- Sometimes people who've encountered death, in particular, feel ready to try limit-stretching activities.

- Some ideas: hang gliding, bungee jumping, skydiving, rock climbing.

- Don't confuse appropriate risk-taking with self-destructiveness. Never test your own mortality through inappropriate behaviors or inadequate safeguards.

CARPE DIEM

Schedule a sunrise hot air balloon ride with a trained, licensed balloonist. Toast the dawn with champagne at 2,000 feet.

60.

PICTURE THIS

- The visual arts have a way of making us see the world anew.

- Perhaps you would enjoy a visit to an art gallery or museum, a sculpture garden, a photography exhibit.

- Why not try to create some art yourself? Attend a watercolor or calligraphy class.

- Making pottery is something almost everyone enjoys. It's tactile and messy and whimsical. Or you could visit a ceramics shop and simply paint pottery that's already been made.

CARPE DIEM

Buy some paints, some brushes and a canvas and paint your feelings about the death. Don't worry about your artistic abilities; just let your imagination take charge. Perhaps paint something you know would bring a smile and a laugh to your brother or sister!

61.

VOLUNTEER

- Consider honoring your sibling's death through social activism. If she died of heart disease, collect money for the American Heart Association. If he had multiple sclerosis, walk in the annual MS walk nearest you.

- My father died from malignant melanoma (the deadliest form of skin cancer). I help sponsor an annual run/walk in my community that raises money to help combat this horrible disease. The contribution I make every year helps me remember my dad and feel like I'm helping prevent similar deaths in the future.

- Volunteer at a local nonprofit, an elementary school, a local hospital—someplace befitting the sibling who died.

- If your schedule is too hectic, offer money instead of time. Make your donation in memory of your sibling.

CARPE DIEM

Call your local United Way and ask for some suggestions about upcoming events you could participate in.

62.

VISIT THE GREAT OUTDOORS

- For many people it is restorative and energizing to spend time outside.

- Mourners often find nature's timeless beauty healing. The sound of a bird singing or the awesome presence of an old tree can help put things in perspective.

- Go on a nature walk. Or camping. Or canoeing. The farther away from civilization the better. Mother Earth knows more about kicking back than all the stress management experts on the planet—and she charges far less.

- Visit someplace outdoors that your sibling once frequented. Yes, you will miss him or her, especially in this setting, but that is more than OK. You miss and you mourn, and as you do so, you begin to ever so slightly heal.

CARPE DIEM

Call your area forest service for a map of nearby walking or hiking trails. Take a hike sometime this week.

63.

SURF THE WEB

- The Web has a number of interesting and informative resources for mourners.

- Many articles about grief are available online. Books can also be purchased online. Most grief organizations now have Web pages. Adult Sibling Grief.com might be a good place for you to start. Visit their website at www.adultsiblinggrief.com. The Compassionate Friends also has adult sibling grief support resources, including links to local chapters. Visit www.compassionatefriends.org.

- Search the words "grief" and "sibling" and see what you find. You may find other blogs or message boards with helpful stories and support from other adult children whose siblings have died.

- Consider setting up your own website and telling your grief story online. You could also use this forum to memorialize your sibling. Personal story websites like these can be poignant and healing both for the poster and the visitor.

CARPE DIEM

Sit down at your computer today and do a search. If you don't own a computer or have access to one at work, visit your local library. Don't forget to visit the Center for Loss website: www.centerforloss.com.

64.

WATCH FOR WARNING SIGNS

- Sometimes mourners fall back on self-destructive behaviors to get through this difficult time.

- Try to be honest with yourself about drug or alcohol abuse. Any kind of addictive behavior that is ultimately self-destructive can be a "red flag" that you need to get some help with your grief. This might include use of drugs or alcohol, gambling, extramarital affairs or difficulties in your work and personal relationships. If you're in over your head, ask someone for help.

- Are you having suicidal thoughts and feelings? Are you isolating yourself too much? Talk to someone today. Let people know you are hurting. They can't read your mind or open your heart.

- Your sibling would want you to get help, not self-destruct!

CARPE DIEM

Acknowledging to ourselves that we have a problem may come too late. If someone suggests that you need help, consider yourself lucky to be so well-loved and get help immediately.

65.

SIMPLIFY YOUR LIFE

- Many of us today are taking stock of what's really important in our lives and trying to discard the rest.

- Mourners are often overwhelmed by all the tasks and commitments we have. If you can rid yourself of some of those extraneous burdens, you'll have more time for mourning and healing.

- What is it that is overburdening you right now? Have your name taken off junk mail lists, ignore your dirty house, stop attending any optional meetings you don't look forward to.

CARPE DIEM

Cancel your newspaper subscription(s) if you're depressed
by what you read. Quit watching TV news for a while.

66.

ESTABLISH A MEMORIAL FUND IN THE NAME OF THE SIBLING WHO DIED

- Sometimes bereaved families ask that memorial contributions be made to specified charities in the name of the person who died. This practice allows friends and family members to show their support while helping the family feel that something good came of the death.

- You can establish a personalized and ongoing memorial to your sibling.

- What was meaningful to your brother or sister? Did she support a certain nonprofit or participate in a certain recreational activity? Was he politically active or affected by a certain illness?

- Your local bank or funeral home may have ideas about how to go about setting up a memorial fund.

- If you mourn well, you will come to a place where you can move forward in honor of your sibling's life, not his or her death.

CARPE DIEM

Call a family member and together brainstorm a list of ideas for a memorial. Suggest that both of you commit to making at least one additional phone call for information before the day is out.

67.

OR CHOOSE TO MEMORIALIZE YOUR SIBLING IN OTHER SPECIAL WAYS

• Setting up a memorial fund is just one way to honor the life of your sibling. Your family may come up with many other creative ideas.

• Consider your sibling's loves and passions. If he were still here, what would make him proud to have his name associated with?

• Some families have set up scholarship funds. Some have donated books to the library or schools. Some have donated park benches or picnic tables, inscribed with an appropriate plaque. Some have planted gardens.

• You might also choose to carry on with something your sibling loved to do or left unfinished.

CARPE DIEM

Ask yourself: What did my sibling really love in life? What was most important to her? How can I keep this love alive?

68.

PREPARE YOURSELF FOR THE HOLIDAYS

- Because your sibling is no longer there to share the holidays with, you may feel particularly sad and vulnerable during Christmas, Easter and other holidays.

- Each holiday has its own history for your family, a history that extends back in time to your childhood. Your family's holiday traditions were formed decades, sometimes centuries, ago and resonate with layer upon layer of memories.

- You probably remember many of the things you and your siblings did together during the holidays, and even memories may now feel painful. Over time, you will come to appreciate your holiday memories again.

- Don't overextend yourself during the holidays. Don't feel you have to shop, bake, entertain, send cards, etc. if you're not up for it.

- Sometimes old holiday rituals are comforting after a death and sometimes they're not. Continue them only if they feel good to you; consider creating new ones, as well.

CARPE DIEM

What's the next major holiday? Make a game plan right now and let those you usually spend the day with know of your plan well in advance.

69.

FIND A GRIEF "BUDDY"

- Though no one else will grieve this death just like you, there are often many others who have had similar experiences. We are rarely totally alone of the path of mourning. Even when there is no guide, there are fellow travelers.

- Find a grief "buddy"—someone who is also mourning the death of a sibling or other loved one, someone you can talk to, someone who also needs a companion in grief right now.

- Make a pact with your grief buddy to call each other whenever one of you needs to talk. Promise to listen without judgment. Commit to spending time together.

- You might arrange to meet once a week for breakfast or lunch with your grief buddy.

CARPE DIEM

Do you know someone who also needs support after the death of someone loved? Call her and ask her out to lunch today. If it feels right, discuss the possibility of being grief buddies.

70.

LIVE FOR BOTH OF YOU

- Your sibling has died, and you are alive. Even though you are grieving and in pain, your life here on earth continues.

- You have a wondrous opportunity: to live and love fully from this moment forward. Has this death made you more aware of the preciousness of our own life?

- You can choose to live in honor of and in memory of your sibling. Find ways to celebrate his or her life, even as you richly live your own. Try some of the activities your sibling loved.

- Be the best you can be.

CARPE DIEM

Finish something your sibling started.

71.

IGNORE HURTFUL ADVICE

- Sometimes well-intentioned but misinformed friends will hurt you unknowingly with their words.

- You may be told:
  - I know how you feel.
  - Get on with your life.
  - Keep your chin up.
  - This is a blessing.
  - Think of all you have to be thankful for.
  - He/she wouldn't want you to be sad.
  - Time heals all wounds.
  - You're strong. You'll get over it.

- Don't take this advice to heart. Such clichés are often offered because people don't know what else to say. The problem is, phrases like these diminish your unique and significant loss.

CARPE DIEM

Consider the clichés you've spoken to mourners in the past in an attempt to comfort them. Forgive yourself just as you should forgive your friends.

72.

MAKE A LIST OF GOALS

- While you should not set a particular time and course for your healing, it may help you to have made other life goals for the coming year.

- Make a list of short-term goals for the next three months. Perhaps some of the goals could have to do with mourning activities (e.g. make a memory book).

- Also make a list of long-term goals for the next year. Be both realistic and compassionate with yourself as you consider what's feasible and feels good and what will only add too much stress to your life.

CARPE DIEM

Write a list of goals for this week. Your goals may be as simple as: Go to work every day. Tell John I love him once a day. Take a walk on Tuesday night.

73.

COUNT YOUR BLESSINGS

- You may not be feeling very good about your life right now. That's OK. There is, indeed, a time for every purpose under heaven.

- Still, you are blessed. Your life has purpose and meaning. It will just take you some time to think and feel this through for yourself.

- Think of all you have to be thankful for. This is not to deny the hurt, for the hurt needs to take precedence right now. But it may help to consider the things that make your life worth living, too.

CARPE DIEM

If you're feeling ready, make a list of the blessings in your life:
your family, your friends, your job, your house. Be specific. "I'm
thankful for Katie's smile. My Wenlock roses. The way the
sun slants through my kitchen window in the morning."

74.

DO SOMETHING YOU'RE GOOD AT

- Often it helps mourners to affirm their worth to others and to themselves.

- Do something you're good at! Ride a bike. Bake a cake. Do the crossword puzzle. Write a poem. Play with your kids. Talk to a friend.

- Have other people told you you're good at this or that? Next time you're complimented in this way, take it to heart! Embrace your gifts that are God-given.

CARPE DIEM

Make a list of ten things you're good at. Do one of them today and afterwards, reflect on how you feel.

75.

IMAGINE YOUR SIBLING IN HEAVEN

- Do you believe in an afterlife? Do you hope that your sibling still exists in some way?

- Most mourners I've talked to—and that number runs into the tens of thousands—are comforted by a belief or a hope that somehow, somewhere, their sibling lives on in health and happiness. For some, this belief is grounded in religious faith. For others it is simply a spiritual sense.

- Some people have dreams in which their sibling seems to be communicating with them. Some feel the overwhelming presence of their sibling on occasion. Some actually "see" or "hear" their sibling. These are common, normal experiences and are often quite comforting.

CARPE DIEM

If you believe in heaven, close your eyes and imagine what it might be like. Imagine your sibling strong and smiling. Imagine him doing what he loves to do in the company of loved ones who have gone before him.

76.

PRACTICE BREATHING IN AND OUT

- After someone we love dies, sometimes what we need most is just to "be." In our goal-oriented society, many of us have lost the knack for simply living.

- Drop all your plans and obligations for today and do nothing.

- Find a quiet place where you can think without distraction and rid your mind of superficial thoughts and concerns. Find someplace quiet, be still, close your eyes and focus on breathing in and out. Relax your muscles. Listen to your own heartbeat.

CARPE DIEM

Try reflecting on this thought: "As I allow myself to mourn, I create an opening in my heart. Releasing the tensions of grief, surrendering to the struggle, means freeing myself to go forward."

77.

TALK OUT LOUD TO THE SIBLING WHO DIED

• Sometimes it feels good to talk to your sibling. Pretend he's sitting in the chair across from you and tell him how you're doing.

• Talk to photos of your sibling. Share your deepest thoughts and feelings with her. Make it part of your daily routine to say "Good morning!" to that photo on your nightstand. (Just be careful who's in earshot! Ha-ha!)

• Visit the cemetery (or columbarium or scattering place if your sibling was cremated) and if you're not too self-conscious, talk to your sister or brother.

• Keep symbols of your sibling around, such as photos or personal belongings that help connect you with the sibling who died. They also help activate your need to mourn.

CARPE DIEM

If you haven't already, put a photo of your sibling in your wallet or purse. Look at it and maybe even talk to it when you're really missing your brother or sister.

78.

DRAW A "GRIEF MAP"

- The death of your sibling may have stirred up all kinds of thoughts and feelings inside you. These thoughts and feelings may seem overwhelming or even "crazy."

- Rest assured that you're not crazy, you're grieving. Your thoughts and feelings—no matter how scary or strange they seem to you—are normal and necessary.

- Sometimes, corralling all your varied thoughts and feelings in one place can make them feel more manageable. You could write about them, but you can also draw them out in diagram form.

- Make a large circle at the center of your map and label it GRIEF. This circle represents your thoughts and feeling since the death. Now draw lines radiating out of this circle and label each line with a thought or feeling that has contributed to your grief. For example, you might write GUILT in a bubble at the end of one line. Next to the word guilt, jot down notes about why you feel guilty.

- Your grief map needn't look pretty or follow any certain rules. The most important thing is the process of creating it. When you're finished, explain it to someone who cares about you.

CARPE DIEM

Stop by your local art supply or hobby shop today and
pick up a large piece of poster board or banner paper. Set
aside an hour or so to work on your grief map today.

79.

SET ASIDE THE ANNIVERSARY OF THE DEATH AS A HOLIDAY

- Perhaps you are not looking forward to the anniversary of your sibling's death. Many adult siblings feel particularly sad and helpless on this day.

- Consider setting aside the anniversary as an annual holiday. Each year, visit your sibling's grave or scattering site. Or plan a ritual activity, such as going on a hike or hosting a family dinner. Perhaps plan a ceremony with friends and family.

- Commemorate the life that was lived by doing something your sibling would have appreciated.

- You might want to spend this day in the company of others who love you.

CARPE DIEM

Call others who loved your sibling and plan an activity for the anniversary of the death.

80.

TALK TO A COUNSELOR

- While grief counseling is not for everyone, many mourners are helped through their grief journeys by a compassionate counselor. It's not indulgent or crazy to see a counselor after a sibling dies—it's simply good self-care!

- If possible, find a counselor who has experience with grief and loss issues.

- Ask your friends for referrals to a counselor they've been helped by.

- Your religious leader may also be a good person to talk to during this time, but only if she affirms your need to mourn this death and search for meaning.

CARPE DIEM

Schedule an initial interview with at least two counselors
so you can see whom you're most comfortable with.

81.

LOOK INTO SUPPORT GROUPS

- Grief support groups are a healing, safe place for many mourners to express their thoughts and feelings. Sharing similar experiences with others who have lost someone loved may help you feel like you're not alone, that you're not going crazy.

- Support groups give you a time and a place—as well as permission—to mourn. They can also help you assess the relationship you had with your sibling and consider the ways in which the death has changed you. Finally, support groups provide you with ideas and choices for reconciling your grief.

- Your local hospice or funeral home may offer a free or low-cost support group.

- If you are newly bereaved, you may not feel ready for a support group. Many mourners are more open to joining a support group 6-9 months after the death. Do what feels right for you.

CARPE DIEM

Call around today for support group information. If you're feeling ready, plan to attend a meeting this week or next.

82.

HELP OTHERS

- Help others! But I'm the one who needs help right now, you may be thinking.

- It's true, you do deserve special compassion and attention right now. But often, people find healing in selflessness.

- Consider volunteering at a nursing home, a homeless shelter, your neighborhood school. Do something your brother or sister would have appreciated.

- If you're well into your grief journey, you may find yourself ready and able to help other mourners by starting a support group or volunteering at a hospice.

- You might even want to plan a trip to my Center for Loss and Life Transition and attend my small group retreat on "Comprehensive Bereavement Skills Training." I'll leave the light on for you! (Visit www.centerforloss.com for information and registration.)

CARPE DIEM

Do something nice for someone else today, maybe
someone who doesn't really deserve it.

83.

TAKE YOUR PHONE OFF THE HOOK
AND UNPLUG THE COMPUTER

- In our hectic lives, the phone is both a can't-live-without-it convenience and an annoying interruption.

- Sometimes we use the phone or e-mail when we should be talking face-to-face.

- Next time you have an urge to call a friend, drop by and visit him instead. Notice how much more intimate and healing it can be to converse in person.

- Don't hide out from yourself or others through the use of any technology. As the Swiss writer Max Frisch has observed, "Technology is the knack of so arranging the world that we do not have to experience it."

CARPE DIEM

Turn your phone off tonight (or silence it). Don't
review your messages until tomorrow.

84.

SAY NO

- Especially soon after the death of your sibling, you may lack the energy as well as the desire to participate in activities you used to find pleasurable. The fancy term for this is "anhedonia," which is the lack of ability to experience pleasure in things you previously found pleasurable. (Next time someone asks how you're doing, just say, "Oh, I'm feeling a bit anhedonistic today" and watch the response you get!)

- It's OK to say no when you're asked to help with a project or attend a party.

- Write a note to the people who've invited you and explain your feelings. Be sure to thank them for the invitation.

- Realize that you can't keep saying no forever. There will always be that first family reunion, birthday party, holiday dinner, etc. Don't miss out on life's most joyful celebrations.

CARPE DIEM

Say no to something today. Allow yourself not to feel guilty about it.

85.

TAKE A MINI-VACATION

- Don't have time to take time off? Plan several mini-vacations this month instead.

- What creative ideas can you come up with to renew yourself? Here are a few ideas to get you started.
  - Schedule a massage with a professional massage therapist
  - Have a spiritual growth weekend. Retreat into nature. Plan some alone time.
  - Go for a drive with no particular destination in mind. Explore the countryside, slow down and observe what you see.
  - Treat yourself to a night in a hotel or bed and breakfast.
  - Visit a museum or a zoo.
  - Go to a yard sale or auction.
  - Go rollerskating or rollerblading with a friend.
  - Drop by a health food store and walk the aisles.

CARPE DIEM

Plan a mini-vacation for today. Spend one
hour doing something special.

86.

RECONNECT WITH
SOMEONE SPECIAL

- Throughout our lives, we often lose contact with people who've touched us or made a difference somehow.

- Death can make us realize that keeping in touch with these people is well worth the effort.

- Whom have you loved or admired but haven't spoken with for a long time?

- Consider teachers, old lovers, childhood friends, past neighbors. Also consider friends and family of your sibling. They may be touched to hear from you.

CARPE DIEM

Write a letter to someone you haven't been in touch with
for a long time. Track down her address and phone
number. Catch her up on your life and invite her to
do the same by calling you or writing you back.

87.

EAT COMFORT FOOD

- Comfort food is food that makes you feel safe, loved, at home; it's often associated with foods we ate as children.

- What foods make you feel this way? What foods did your family particularly enjoy? When you were a child, what was your favorite dinner?

- Did you have a favorite food you and your sibling both enjoyed?

- Some examples: macaroni and cheese, mashed potatoes, chicken soup, hot cocoa laden with tiny marshmallows.

CARPE DIEM

Tonight, in honor of your sibling, prepare your
favorite childhood meal for your family.

88.

REMEMBER OTHERS WHO HAD A SPECIAL RELATIONSHIP WITH YOUR SIBLING

- At times your appropriately inward focus will make you feel alone in your grief. But you're not alone. There are probably many other people who loved and miss your sibling.

- Think about others who were affected by your sibling's death: friends, neighbors, distant relatives, children, grandchildren.

- Is there someone outside of the primary "circle of mourners" who may be struggling with this death? Perhaps you could call her and offer your condolences.

CARPE DIEM

Today, write and mail a brief supportive note to
someone else affected by the death. If you aren't a
writer, give them a call or stop in for a visit.

89.

SCHEDULE SOMETHING THAT GIVES YOU PLEASURE EACH AND EVERY DAY

- Often mourners need something to look forward to, a reason to get out of bed today.

- It's hard to look forward to each day when you know you will be experiencing pain and sadness.

- To counterbalance your normal and necessary mourning, plan something you enjoy doing every day.

- Reading, baking, going for a walk, having lunch with a friend, gardening, playing computer games—whatever brings you enjoyment.

CARPE DIEM

What's on tap for today? Squeeze in something you enjoy, no matter how hectic your schedule.

90.

TEACH OTHERS ABOUT GRIEF AND MOURNING

- To love is to one day mourn. You have learned this most poignant of life's lessons.

- Maybe you could teach what you are learning to others. Tell your friends and family about the six needs of mourning. Teach them how they can best support you.

- Teach your children about mourning and help them mourn the death of their aunt or uncle. Provide them with mourning opportunities and activities. Model your own grief and mourning openly and honestly. Whatever you do, don't hide your grief in an effort to protect your children. This will teach them to hide their feelings, too.

- Share your wisdom in the safety of a grief support group.

- Remember that each person's grief is unique. Your experiences will not be shared or appreciated by everyone.

CARPE DIEM

Buy a friend the companion book to this one, called *Healing A Friend's Grieving Heart: 100 Practical Ideas for Helping Someone You Love Through Loss*. It provides concise grief education and practical tips for helping.

91.

MEDITATE

- Meditation invites your body into a more relaxed physical state, lowers your blood pressure, increases oxygen circulation, improves your immune system, increases your ability to concentrate, calms your mind, and stimulates an overall feeling of well-being.

- Give yourself five full minutes to concentrate on your breathing. Breathe from your diaphragm; push your stomach out as you breathe in and pull your stomach in as you breathe out. Imagine that you're inhaling the spiritual energy you need to help you integrate loss into your life and that you're exhaling your feelings of sadness and grief. No, this doesn't make your grief go away, but it helps soothe your soul.

- Breathing opens you up. Grief may have naturally closed you down. The power of breath helps to fill your empty spaces. The old wisdom of "count to ten" is all about taking a breath to open up space for something to happen. The paradox is that in slowing down you create diving momentum that invites you to continue to mourn.

- There are many resources available to help you learn how to meditate. One of my personal favorites is a classic simply titled *How to Meditate*, by Lawrence LeShan. Learning to meditate can give you a new understanding of your grief journey and your life journey. Meditation trains you to descend to a level of peace and calm. The more you meditate, the greater your self understanding becomes, and the more you re-light your divine spark.

CARPE DIEM

Make a commitment right now to learn how to meditate. Pick up the book noted above within the next several days. Just a few minutes of meditation each day will provide you a wonderful spiritual perspective on where you are in your life's journey.

92.

CREATE A SANCTUARY JUST FOR YOU

- Mourners need safe places they can go when they feel ready to embrace their grief.

- Create a sanctuary in your own home, a retreat that's just for you. Furnish it with a comfy chair, reading materials, a journal, a music player. No TV. Or, you may want this to be a room dedicated to silence. As Thomas Moore has noted, "Silence allows many sounds to reach awareness that otherwise would be unheard."

- An outside "room" can be equally effective. Do you have a porch or patio where you can just "be"? Locate a comfortable chair and install a tabletop fountain.

- Your sanctuary, even if just a simple room, can become a place dedicated exclusively to the needs of the soul. The death of your sibling requires "soul work." Your creation of a sanctuary honors that reality.

CARPE DIEM

Identify a spot in your house that can be your
sanctuary. Begin readying it today.

93.

SLEEP TIGHT

- Mourning is fatiguing work. Feelings of exhaustion and low energy are extremely common.

- Your body is telling you it needs rest, so indulge your fatigue. Schedule at least eight hours of slumber into your day. Develop a relaxing bedtime routine so you're ready for sleep.

- Buy yourself new bedding and a good new pillow—or hang onto an old pillow that has always brought you comfort.

- Lie down for short rest periods periodically throughout the day. Take an afternoon nap if you feel like it.

- If you feel you are "oversleeping," see your doctor. Sometimes this can be a symptom of a more severe depression. I often say, "When in doubt, get checked out."

CARPE DIEM

Tonight, begin getting ready for bed right after dinner. Take your phone off the hook, bathe or shower, listen to soothing music, sip hot herbal tea in bed as you read a good book or write in your journal.

94.

VISIT THE CEMETERY OR SCATTERING SITE

- Visiting the cemetery is an important mourning ritual. It helps us embrace our loss and remember those who have died.

- Memorial Day, Veteran's Day, Labor Day, and holidays are traditional days to visit the cemetery and pay respects. You might also want to spend time at the gravesite on your brother or sister's birthday.

- If your sibling's body was cremated, you may want to visit the scattering site or columbarium.

- Ask a friend or family member to go with you. You may feel comforted by their presence. On the other hand, you may find it more meaningful to go by yourself. At times, your aloneness may help you feel closer to your sibling.

CARPE DIEM

If you can, drop by the cemetery today with a nosegay
of fresh flowers. Scatter the petals over the grave.

95.

TAKE SOME TIME OFF WORK

- Typically, our society grants us three days "bereavement leave" and then expects us to return to work as if nothing happened.

- As you know, three days is a paltry allowance for grief. Talk to your supervisor about taking off some additional time following your sibling's death. Some companies will grant extended leaves of absence or sabbaticals in some situations.

- If you simply can't take off additional time, request that your work load be lightened for the next several months.

- On the other hand, the routine of work comforts some mourners. Returning to work and to co-workers who care about you may be just what you need—so long as you're not overworking in an attempt—conscious or subconscious—to avoid your grief.

CARPE DIEM

Take a mental health day today and call in sick. Spend the day resting or doing something you enjoy.

96.

LET GO OF DESTRUCTIVE MYTHS ABOUT GRIEF AND MOURNING

- Unknowingly, you have probably internalized many of our society's harmful myths about grief and mourning.

- Here are some to let go of:
    - I need to be strong and carry on.
    - Tears are a sign of weakness.
    - I need to get over my grief.
    - Death is something we don't talk about.

- Sometimes these myths will cause you to feel guilty about or ashamed of your true thoughts and feelings.

- Your grief is your grief. It's normal and necessary. Allow it to be what it is. Allow it to last as long as it lasts. Strive to be an authentic mourner—one who openly and honestly expresses what you think and feel.

CARPE DIEM

De-mythologize grief in your house by talking to your family about grief and mourning. Let them know that their feelings about your sibling's death are normal and necessary. Share how you've been feeling.

97.

GET AWAY FROM IT ALL

- Sometimes it takes a change of scenery to reveal the texture of our lives.

- New people and places help us see our lives from a new vantage point and can assist us in our search for meaning.

- Often, getting away from it all means leaving civilization behind and retreating to nature. But it can also mean temporarily abandoning your environment and spending time in one that's altogether different.

- Visit a foreign country. Go backpacking in the wilderness. Spend a weekend at a monastery. Is there someplace your sibling always dreamed of visiting but never did? Maybe you can travel there on his behalf.

- In the Bible, the career of Abraham begins with God saying, "Go forth." An alternative translation of the Hebrew is "Go to yourself." The practice of voluntary exile was actually designed to humble oneself and remind oneself that everything comes from God.

CARPE DIEM

Plan a trip to somewhere far away. Ask a friend to travel with you.

98.

REASSESS YOUR PRIORITIES

- Death has a way of making us rethink our lives and the meaningfulness of the ways we spend them.

- The death of a sibling often challenges us to consider our own lives and deaths. You've witnessed a life come to an end. Was it a rich, loving, satisfying life? What can you learn from your sibling's life and death?

- What gives your life meaning? What doesn't? Take steps to spend more of your time on the former and less on the latter.

- Now may be the time to reconfigure your life. Choose a satisfying new career. Go back to school. Begin volunteering. Move closer to your family. Be kinder and more compassionate.

CARPE DIEM

Imagine yourself five years from now. What is your life like?
How do you feel about the death of your sibling? Is your future
what you hoped it would be? How can you begin to make
changes now so that your life will become what you wish?

99.

UNDERSTAND THE CONCEPT OF "RECONCILIATION"

- Sometimes you'll hear about mourners "recovering" from grief. This term is damaging because it implies that grief is an illness that must be cured. It also connotes a return to the way things were before the death.

- Mourners don't recover from grief. We become "reconciled" to it. In other words, we learn to live with it and are forever changed by it.

- This does not mean a life of misery, however. Mourners often not only heal but grow through grief. Our lives can potentially be deeper and more meaningful after the death of someone loved.

- Reconciliation takes time. You may not become truly reconciled to your loss for several years and even then will have "griefbursts" (see Idea 53) forever.

- I believe every human being wants to "mourn well" the deaths of those they love. It is as essential as breathing. Some people make the choice to give momentum to their mourning, while others deny or avoid it. The path you choose to take will make all the difference. Move toward your grief and go on to live until you die!

CARPE DIEM

Write down the following definition of reconciliation and post it somewhere you will see it often: I am learning to integrate my grief into my life. I will not "get over" my grief, but if I do the necessary work of mourning, I will go on to live a joyful life.

100.

BELIEVE IN YOUR CAPACITY TO HEAL AND GROW THROUGH GRIEF

- In time, you may find that you are growing emotionally and spiritually as a result of your grief journey.

- Growth means a new inner balance with no end points. Your life will never be exactly the same as it was when your sibling was still alive.

- Growth means exploring our assumptions about life. Ultimately, exploring our assumptions about life after the death of someone loved can make those assumptions richer and more life-affirming.

- Growth means utilizing our potentials. The encounter of grief reawakens us to the importance of utilizing our potentials—our capacities to mourn our losses openly and without shame, to be interpersonally effective in our relationships with others, and to continue to discover fulfillment in life, living and loving.

CARPE DIEM

Consider the ways in which you may be growing
since the death of your sibling.

A FINAL WORD

"Our brothers and sisters are there with us from the dawn of our personal stories to the inevitable dusk."
—Susan Scarf Merrell

In the beginning of this book, I acknowledged that to be "bereaved" means "to be torn apart" and to have "special needs." One of your most important needs is to practice excellent self-care during this time. I hope the self-care principles outlined in this resource will help fortify you for the ongoing ebbs and flows of your grief journey. When we recognize that excellent self-care is anchored in having the courage to mourn, we allow ourselves to begin to heal, and that is self-care at its very best.

As Amy Anderson said in the Foreword, she lost her "best friend, confidant, and partner in crime." With the death of her precious brother, Mitch, her future changed, her past changed, her life changed, her everything changed. Like Amy, you too have been forever changed by the death of your brother or sister.

Your commitment to surrender to your grief is an integral part of your ultimate healing. Then and only then do you go on to find meaning and purpose in your continued living. Oh, but once you have the courage and fortitude to do your work of mourning, your open and grateful heart will fill your soul with love and light!

Yes, it takes patience to discover life again after the death of a sibling. And it takes self-compassion to believe that putting the principles explored in this book into action will actually help the pain of your loss soften over time.

I truly hope this little book has served and will continue to serve as a gentle companion to you. Right now, take a moment to close your eyes, open your heart, and remember the lovely smile of your brother or sister.

Bless you. I wish you peace.

THE MOURNER'S CODE

Ten Self-Compassionate Principles

Though you should reach out to others as you journey through grief, you should not feel obligated to accept the unhelpful responses you may receive from some people. You are the one who is grieving, and as such, you have certain "rights" no one should try to take away from you.

The following list is intended both to empower you to heal and to decide how others can and cannot help. This is not to discourage you from reaching out to others for help, but rather to assist you in distinguishing useful responses from hurtful ones.

1. **You have the right to experience your own unique grief.** No one else will grieve in exactly the same way you do. So, when you turn to others for help, don't allow them to tell you what you should or should not be feeling.

2. **You have the right to talk about your grief.** Talking about your grief will help you heal. Seek out others who will allow you to talk as much as you want, as often as you want, about your grief. If at times you don't feel like talking, you also have the right to be silent.

3. **You have the right to feel a multitude of emotions.** Confusion, numbness, disorientation, fear, guilt and relief are just a few of the emotions you might feel as part of your grief journey. Others may try to tell you that feeling angry, for example, is wrong. Don't take these judgmental responses to heart. Instead, find listeners who will accept your feelings without condition.

4. **You have the right to be tolerant of your physical and emotional limits.** Your feelings of loss and sadness will probably leave you feeling fatigued. Respect what your body and mind are telling you. Get daily rest. Eat balanced meals. And don't allow others to push you into doing things you don't feel ready to do.

5. **You have the right to experience "griefbursts."** Sometimes, out of nowhere, a powerful surge of grief may overcome you. This can be frightening, but it is normal and natural. Find someone who understands and will let you talk it out.

6. **You have the right to make use of ritual.** The funeral ritual does more than acknowledge the death of someone loved. It helps provide you with the support of caring people. More importantly, the funeral is a way for you to mourn. If others tell you the funeral or other healing rituals such as these are silly or unnecessary, don't listen.

7. **You have the right to embrace your spirituality.** If faith is a part of your life, express it in ways that seem appropriate to you. Allow yourself to be around people who understand and support your religious beliefs. If you feel angry at God, find someone to talk with who won't be critical of your feelings of hurt and abandonment.

8. **You have the right to search for meaning.** You may find yourself asking, "Why did he or she die? Why this way? Why now?" Some of your questions may have answers, but some may not. And watch out for the clichéd responses some people may give you. Comments like, "It was God's will" or "Think of what you have to be thankful for" are not helpful and you do not have to accept them.

9. **You have the right to treasure your memories.** Memories are one of the best legacies that exist after the death of someone loved. You will always remember. Instead of ignoring your memories, find others with whom you can share them.

10. **You have the right to move toward your grief and heal.** Reconciling your grief will not happen quickly. Remember, grief is a process, not an event. Be patient and tolerant with yourself and avoid people who are impatient and intolerant with you. Neither you nor those around you must forget that the death of someone loved changes your life forever.

SEND US YOUR IDEAS FOR HEALING THE ADULT SIBLING'S GRIEVING HEART!

I'd love to hear your practical ideas for being self-compassionate in grief. I may use them in future editions of this book or in other publications through the Center for Loss. Please jot down your ideas and mail them to:

Dr. Alan Wolfelt
The Center for Loss and Life Transition
3735 Broken Bow Road
Fort Collins, CO 80526
DrWolfelt@centerforloss.com

I look forward to hearing from you!

My idea:

_____

_____

_____

_____

My name and mailing address:

_____

_____

_____

ALSO BY ALAN WOLFELT

The Wilderness of Grief
Finding Your Way

A beautiful, hardcover gift book version of
Understanding Your Grief

Understanding Your Grief provides a comprehensive
exploration of grief and the ten essential touchstones
for finding hope and healing your heart. *The Wilderness
of Grief* is an excerpted version of *Understanding Your
Grief*, making it approachable and appropriate for all mourners.

This concise book makes an excellent gift for anyone in mourning. On the
book's inside front cover is room for writing an inscription to your grieving
friend.

While some readers will appreciate the more in-depth *Understanding
Your Grief*, others may feel overwhelmed by the amount of information it
contains. For these readers we recommend *The Wilderness of Grief*. (Fans of
Understanding Your Grief will also want a copy of *The Wilderness of Grief* to
turn to in spare moments.)

The Wilderness of Grief is an ideal book for the bedside or coffee table. Pick
it up before bed and read just a few pages. You'll be carried off to sleep by its
gentle, affirming messages of hope and healing.

ISBN 978-1-879651-52-4 • 128 pages • hardcover • $15.95

All Dr. Wolfelt's publications can be ordered by mail from:
Companion Press
3735 Broken Bow Road
Fort Collins, CO 80526
(970) 226-6050
www.centerforloss.com

ALSO BY ALAN WOLFELT

Understanding Your Grief

Ten Essential Touchstones for Finding Hope and Healing Your Heart

One of North America's leading grief educators, Dr. Alan Wolfelt has written many books about healing in grief. This book is his most comprehensive, covering the essential lessons that mourners have taught him in his three decades of working with the bereaved.

In compassionate, down-to-earth language, *Understanding Your Grief* describes ten touchstones—or trail markers—that are essential physical, emotional, cognitive, social, and spiritual signs for mourners to look for on their journey through grief.

The Ten Essential Touchstones:

1. Open to the presence of your loss.
2. Dispel misconceptions about grief.
3. Embrace the uniqueness of your grief.
4. Explore what you might experience.
5. Recognize you are not crazy.
6. Understand the six needs of mourning.
7. Nurture yourself.
8. Reach out for help.
9. Seek reconciliation, not resolution.
10. Appreciate your transformation.

Think of your grief as a wilderness—a vast, inhospitable forest. You must journey through this wilderness. To find your way out, you must become acquainted with its terrain and learn to follow the sometimes hard-to-find trail that leads to healing. In the wilderness of your grief, the touchstones are your trail markers. They are the signs that let you know you are on the right path. When you learn to identify and rely on the touchstones, you will find your way to hope and healing.

ISBN 978-1-879651-35-7 • 176 pages • softcover • $14.95

All Dr. Wolfelt's publications can be ordered by mail from:
Companion Press
3735 Broken Bow Road
Fort Collins, CO 80526
(970) 226-6050
www.centerforloss.com

ALSO BY ALAN WOLFELT

The Understanding Your Grief Journal

Exploring the Ten Essential Touchstones

Writing can be a very effective form of mourning, or expressing your grief outside yourself. And it is through mourning that you heal in grief.

The Understanding Your Grief Journal is a companion workbook to Dr. Wolfelt's *Understanding Your Grief.* Designed to help mourners explore the many facets of their unique grief through journaling, this compassionate book interfaces with the ten essential touchstones. Throughout, journalers are asked specific questions about their own unique grief journeys as they relate to the touchstones and are provided with writing space for the many questions asked.

Purchased as a set together with *Understanding Your Grief*, this journal is a wonderful mourning tool and safe place for those in grief. It also makes an ideal grief support group workbook.

ISBN 978-1-879651-39-5 • 150 pages • softcover • $14.95

All Dr. Wolfelt's publications can be ordered by mail from:
Companion Press
3735 Broken Bow Road
Fort Collins, CO 80526
(970) 226-6050
www.centerforloss.com

ALSO BY ALAN WOLFELT

Living in the Shadow of the Ghosts of Grief
Step into the Light
Reconcile old losses and open the door to infinite joy and love

"*Accumulated, unreconciled loss affects every aspect of our lives.* Living in the Shadow *is a beautifully written compass with the needle ever-pointing in the direction of hope.*"
— Greg Yoder, grief counselor

"*So often we try to dance around our grief. This book offers the reader a safe place to do the healing work of "catch-up" mourning, opening the door to a life of freedom, authenticity and purpose.*"
— Kim Farris-Luke, bereavement coordinator

Are you depressed? Anxious? Angry? Do you have trouble with trust and intimacy? Do you feel a lack of meaning and purpose in your life? You may well be living in the shadow of the ghosts of grief.

When you suffer a loss of any kind—whether through abuse, divorce, job loss, the death of someone loved or other transitions, you naturally grieve inside. To heal your grief, you must express it. That is, you must mourn your grief. If you don't, you will carry your grief into your future, and it will undermine your happiness for the rest of your life.

This compassionate guide will help you learn to identify and mourn your carried grief so you can go on to live the joyful, whole life you deserve.

ISBN 978-1-879651-51-7 • 160 pages • softcover • $13.95

All Dr. Wolfelt's publications can be ordered by mail from:
Companion Press
3735 Broken Bow Road
Fort Collins, CO 80526
(970) 226-6050
www.centerforloss.com

ALSO BY ALAN WOLFELT

The Journey Through Grief

Reflections On Healing
Second Edition

This popular hardcover book makes a wonderful gift for those who grieve, helping them gently engage in the work of mourning. Comforting and nurturing, *The Journey Through Grief* doses mourners with the six needs of mourning, helping them soothe themselves at the same time it helps them heal.

Back by popular demand, we are now offering *The Journey Through Grief* again in hardcover. The hardcover version of this beautiful book makes a wonderful, healing gift for the newly bereaved.

This revised, second edition of *The Journey Through Grief* takes Dr. Wolfelt's popular book of reflections and adds space for guided journaling, asking readers thoughtful questions about their unique mourning needs and providing room to write responses.

The Journey Through Grief is organized around the six needs that all mourners must yield to—indeed embrace—if they are to go on to find continued meaning in life and living. Following a short explanation of each mourning need is a series of brief, spiritual passages that, when read slowly and reflectively, help mourners work through their unique thoughts and feelings. *The Journey Through Grief* is being used by many faith communities as part of their grief support programs.

ISBN 978-1-879651-11-1 • hardcover • 176 pages • $21.95

All Dr. Wolfelt's publications can be ordered by mail from:
Companion Press
3735 Broken Bow Road
Fort Collins, CO 80526
(970) 226-6050
www.centerforloss.com